TITLE: "INEXPERIENC E, BUT NOT INCOMPETENT"

CONTENTS

Chapter One

Introduction

In the world of hiring, experience has long been considered the Holy Grail, the golden ticket that unlocks the door to success. Recruiters pore over résumés, meticulously scanning for those coveted years of experience, as if they alone guarantee competence and proficiency. But what if we've been looking at it all wrong?

This book, "Inexperience, but not Incompetent: Unleashing the Potential of New Talent," challenges the prevailing notion that experience is the sole indicator of a candidate's abilities It invites recruiters and hiring managers to explore an alternative approach, one that recognizes the untapped potential in individuals who may lack experience but possess other invaluable qualities.

Let's face it: experience is not always a reliable gauge of competence. How many times have you encountered seasoned professionals who fail to meet expectations, while someone with less experience but a burning desire to learn shines brightly? We must acknowledge that experience alone does not guarantee success.

By opening our minds and embracing a paradigm shift, we can redefine the hiring process and unleash the true potential of new talent. This begins with offering candidates an opportunity to showcase their abilities during a probationary period, typically lasting two weeks.

During this time, employers can observe how candidates adapt to the new role, evaluate their willingness to learn, and assess their potential for growth. This approach allows for a more holistic assessment, focusing not just on past experiences, but also on traits like motivation, adaptability, and a hunger for knowledge.

Throughout the pages of this book, we will explore the myths surrounding experience-based hiring. We will delve into real-life stories and examples that challenge the status quo and demonstrate the limitations of a solely experience-driven approach. By doing so, we hope to inspire recruiters and hiring managers to embrace change and unlock the untapped potential in individuals who may not have lengthy résumés but possess the drive and determination to succeed.

Together, we will uncover strategies to identify candidates who are willing to learn, grow, and contribute meaningfully to their roles and organizations. We will discuss how to design effective onboarding programs that foster growth and development. And we will address the challenges that may arise, equipping you with the tools to overcome resistance and objections.

It is time to shift our focus from mere experience to the potential lying dormant within every individual. It is time to build a culture that values motivation, curiosity, and a hunger for growth. Are you ready to embark on this transformative journey?

Join us as we dive into the world of hiring beyond experience, a world where the inexperienced, but not incompetent, have the opportunity to prove their worth. Together, let's create a more inclusive and forward-thinking approach to talent acquisition and unleash the full potential of new talent.

Chapter two

The Myth of Experience

The allure of experience is deeply ingrained in our collective mindset. It seems only natural to assume that someone with years of experience in a specific field would be the most qualified candidate for a job. After all, experience often equates to knowledge, right?

But let us challenge this long-standing assumption and unravel the myth of experience.

Experience does have its merits. It can provide valuable insights, honed skills, and the ability to navigate familiar situations with ease. However, it is essential to recognize that experience is not a foolproof indicator of competence or future success.

Consider this scenario: A candidate with a decade of experience in a particular industry applies for a position. Their résumé brims with accomplishments and accolades. Yet, upon joining the company, they struggle to adapt to new processes, resist change, and find themselves stuck in old habits. Despite their wealth of experience, they struggle to perform at the level expected.

Conversely, picture a candidate who is new to the industry but displays an insatiable hunger to learn and grow. They bring fresh perspectives, unburdened by preconceived notions and rigid routines. They embrace challenges as opportunities for growth and approach each task with enthusiasm. Given the chance, they quickly surpass expectations and contribute to the organization's success.

These examples highlight the fallacy of assuming that experience alone guarantees competence. Experience is just one piece of the puzzle, and it is essential to consider other factors when evaluating a candidate's potential.

By fixating solely on experience, we risk overlooking individuals who possess the drive, determination, and capacity for growth that are vital for success in today's rapidly evolving world. We must acknowledge that the world is changing at an unprecedented pace, and experience alone may not equip individuals with the agility and adaptability necessary to thrive in dynamic environments.

Moreover, relying solely on experience perpetuates bias and limits diversity in the workplace. It reinforces the status quo, favoring those who have had access to opportunities and privileges that allowed them to accumulate experience. By broadening our perspective and considering alternative criteria, we can foster a more inclusive hiring process that values potential, passion, and a hunger to learn.

Imagine the possibilities if we shifted our mindset, placing greater emphasis on candidates' willingness to learn, their adaptability, and their eagerness to contribute. We would create a workforce filled with individuals who embrace change, constantly seek improvement, and are unafraid to challenge the status quo.

In the following chapters, we will explore practical strategies for identifying and assessing these valuable traits during the hiring process. We will examine ways to overcome the biases that often accompany experience-based hiring decisions. Together, we will uncover the untapped potential within individuals who may be inexperienced but possess the drive and determination to excel.

It is time to question the myth of experience and embrace a more holistic approach to talent acquisition. Let us venture beyond the confines of tradition and discover the true potential that lies within every individual, regardless of their experience level.

Chapter Three

Redefining Hiring Criteria

The traditional hiring process heavily relies on résumés, with experience as the primary determining factor for selecting candidates. However, it is time to challenge this narrow perspective and redefine our hiring criteria. By embracing a more inclusive approach, we can unlock the potential of new talent and create a workforce that thrives on growth and adaptability.

Enter the concept of the probationary period—a period of approximately two weeks during which candidates have the opportunity to prove themselves in the new role. This approach allows employers to evaluate candidates based on their performance, learning agility, and potential for growth, rather than solely on their prior experience.

During the probationary period, candidates have the chance to immerse themselves in the organization's culture, interact with team members, and get hands-on experience with the tasks and responsibilities of the role. This period serves as an invaluable opportunity for both the employer and the candidate to assess their fit within the organization and evaluate their long-term potential.

By shifting the focus from experience to potential, recruiters can identify candidates who demonstrate the qualities and skills necessary for success. Let's explore some of these key qualities:

1. ***Motivation and Drive:*** Look for candidates who exhibit a genuine enthusiasm for the role and a passion for learning. Assess their willingness to go the extra mile, take initiative, and tackle challenges head-on. Motivation is a powerful driver of success, as it fuels continuous improvement and a desire for excellence.

2. ***Adaptability and Flexibility:*** In today's fast-paced and ever-changing world, adaptability is a crucial skill. Seek candidates who demonstrate a willingness to embrace change, navigate uncertainty, and quickly learn new skills. Their ability to adapt and thrive in evolving circumstances will prove invaluable to the organization's growth.

3. ***Curiosity and Hunger for Knowledge:*** Curiosity is the fuel that drives learning and innovation. Look for candidates who exhibit a genuine thirst for knowledge, ask thoughtful questions, and actively seek opportunities to expand their

understanding. These individuals are more likely to approach their work with a growth mindset and continually seek ways to improve.

4. ***Communication and Collaboration:*** Effective communication and collaboration are vital for success in any role. Observe how candidates interact with others during the probationary period. Are they able to communicate their ideas clearly? Do they actively listen and contribute to team discussions? Strong interpersonal skills are indicative of a candidate's potential to collaborate effectively within the organization.

During the probationary period, employers can evaluate candidates based on these qualities, providing a more comprehensive and accurate assessment of their potential. It is essential to structure this period with clear expectations and feedback mechanisms, allowing candidates to understand what is expected of them and providing guidance for improvement.

By redefining our hiring criteria and embracing the potential of new talent, we open doors for individuals who may not have extensive experience but possess the drive, motivation, and eagerness to learn. Through this approach, organizations can build diverse and dynamic teams that thrive on continuous growth and innovation.

In the next chapter, we will explore practical strategies for identifying these qualities in candidates and creating an effective onboarding process that nurtures their potential. Let us embark on a journey of reimagining talent acquisition, where potential is valued alongside experience, and growth becomes the foundation of success.

Chapter Four

The Power of Willingness to Learn

Personal Experience: A Journey of Growth and Opportunity

In my pursuit of a job as a fresh college graduate in the year 2016, I faced numerous rejections from recruiters who were fixated on the need for prior job experience. It seemed like an insurmountable barrier, leaving me questioning my own worth and potential. However, my story took a turn when I was offered a chance at Makac Global, an organization specializing in online registration for Jamb examinations.

My lack of experience and digital skills meant that I was placed under a probationary period of one week. It was during this time that I was given the opportunity to prove my capabilities, to demonstrate that despite my inexperience, I possessed the drive and determination to learn and contribute.

The probationary training opened doors for me. In less than four days, my boss recognized that he had made the right choice in giving me a chance. I quickly transformed into a powerhouse within Makac Global Integrated, exceeding expectations and making a significant impact.

This personal experience serves as a testament to the power of willingness to learn. While my lack of experience could have been seen as a disadvantage, it was my eagerness to grow, adapt, and embrace new challenges that ultimately led to my success.

In a world that often overlooks the potential of those without experience, it is crucial to recognize that giving individuals a chance can unlock hidden talent. My story is not unique, as there are countless individuals who possess the same hunger for knowledge and willingness to learn, waiting for an opportunity to prove themselves.

It is time to shift our focus from the constraints of experience and start valuing these qualities—motivation, adaptability, and a growth mindset as essential criteria in the hiring process. By doing so, we create space for the untapped potential of individuals who may lack experience but possess the drive and determination to excel.

By incorporating probationary periods into the hiring process, organizations can provide a platform for candidates to showcase their skills and adaptability. It is during this period that hidden talents can be unearthed, and individuals can prove their worth beyond what their résumés may suggest.

My personal journey highlights the transformative power of giving individuals a chance to learn and grow. It is a reminder that experience is not the sole determinant of success. The willingness to learn, coupled with a supportive environment that fosters growth, can turn an inexperienced individual into a valuable asset for any organization.

In the upcoming chapters, we will delve deeper into the strategies for identifying and nurturing this potential during the hiring process. We will explore the importance of creating a supportive onboarding program that empowers individuals to thrive, regardless of their prior experience. Together, let us continue to unravel the untapped potential of new talent and reshape the hiring landscape.

Chapter Five

Designing Effective Onboarding Programs

The journey of unlocking the potential of new talent does not end with the hiring process alone. It extends into the critical phase of onboarding, where organizations have the opportunity to nurture and develop the skills and capabilities of their new hires. In this chapter, we will explore the key elements of designing effective onboarding programs that foster growth and unleash the full potential of individuals, regardless of their prior experience.

1. *Clear Expectations and Goals:* A successful onboarding program begins with setting clear expectations and goals for

new hires. Clearly communicate the responsibilities and objectives of their role, outlining the skills and knowledge they are expected to develop over time. This clarity provides a foundation for growth and allows individuals to understand what is expected of them from the start.

2. ***Mentorship and Guidance:*** Assigning mentors or experienced team members to guide and support new hires can be immensely valuable. Mentors can share their knowledge, provide feedback, and help new hires navigate the intricacies of the organization. This mentorship fosters a culture of learning and creates a support system for individuals to lean on during their early days in the company.

3. ***Ongoing Training and Development:*** Recognize that learning is a continuous process, and provide opportunities for new hires to acquire new skills and expand their knowledge base. Implement regular training sessions, workshops, and access to relevant resources to facilitate their growth. By investing in their development, organizations create an environment that encourages continuous learning and improvement.

4. *Feedback and Performance Evaluation:* Regular feedback and performance evaluations are crucial during the onboarding phase. Provide constructive feedback to new hires, highlighting their strengths and areas for improvement. This feedback loop encourages growth, allows for course correction, and helps individuals align their actions with organizational goals. It also demonstrates that the organization is invested in their success.

5. *Encourage Collaboration and Cross-functional Exposure:* Foster a collaborative environment where new hires have opportunities to work with different teams and departments. This exposure helps them gain a broader understanding of the organization, enhances their problem-solving skills, and encourages cross-functional collaboration. By breaking down silos and promoting collaboration, organizations tap into the collective intelligence and diverse perspectives of their workforce.

6. *Celebrate Milestones and Achievements:* Recognize and celebrate the milestones and achievements of new hires during their onboarding journey. Acknowledge their growth,

contributions, and milestones reached, as this reinforces their confidence and motivation. Celebrations can take the form of team recognition, awards, or even simple expressions of appreciation. Such gestures foster a positive onboarding experience and create a sense of belonging within the organization.

By incorporating these elements into the design of onboarding programs, organizations can create an environment that nurtures the potential of new talent. The focus shifts from relying solely on prior experience to investing in the growth and development of individuals, recognizing that their potential lies beyond what is written on their résumés.

In the next chapter, we will address the challenges that organizations may face when adopting this alternative approach to hiring and onboarding. We will provide strategies for overcoming resistance, addressing biases, and fostering a culture that values potential and growth. Together, let us pave the way for a more inclusive and forward-thinking approach to talent acquisition and development.

Chapter Six

Overcoming Challenges and Building a Culture of Potential

Implementing a hiring and onboarding process that values potential over experience may face resistance from traditional norms and biases deeply ingrained in the organizational culture. In this chapter, we will address these challenges and provide strategies for building a culture that embraces the untapped potential of individuals, creating a dynamic and inclusive workforce.

1. ***Overcoming Bias:*** Recognize and challenge the biases that can hinder the adoption of a potential-focused approach. Biases based on age, educational background, or lack of experience can limit opportunities for individuals with immense potential. Encourage diversity and inclusion by actively seeking out candidates from different backgrounds and experiences. Foster a culture that values diverse perspectives and acknowledges the potential that lies within each individual.

2. ***Educating Recruiters and Hiring Managers:*** Provide training and education to recruiters and hiring managers about the benefits of valuing potential. Help them understand how to assess qualities such as motivation, adaptability, and a

growth mindset during the hiring process. Equip them with the tools and knowledge needed to recognize and cultivate potential in candidates.

3. *Implementing Objective Assessments:* Supplement traditional interviews and résumé screenings with objective assessments that gauge a candidate's potential. Use situational judgment tests, problem-solving exercises, or case studies to evaluate a candidate's ability to adapt, learn, and think critically. These assessments provide a more holistic view of a candidate's potential beyond their prior experience.

4. *Cultivating a Learning Culture:* Foster a culture of continuous learning and growth within the organization. Encourage employees to pursue professional development opportunities, offer mentorship programs, and provide access to learning resources. By demonstrating a commitment to growth and learning, organizations inspire employees to continually develop their skills and unlock their potential.

5. *Recognizing and Rewarding Growth:* Establish mechanisms to recognize and reward employees who demonstrate exceptional growth and performance. Highlight success

stories of individuals who have thrived despite limited prior experience. Celebrate their achievements and showcase their journey as inspiration for others. By highlighting the value of growth and potential, organizations reinforce the importance of these qualities in the workplace.

6. ***Refining and Iterating the Process:*** Continuously evaluate and refine the hiring and onboarding processes to optimize the identification and cultivation of potential. Seek feedback from new hires, mentors, and team members to understand their experiences and make necessary adjustments. Embrace a mindset of constant improvement and adaptability in creating a culture that values and nurtures potential.

By addressing these challenges head-on and implementing these strategies, organizations can build a culture that values potential and growth. They can create an environment where individuals are given the opportunity to prove themselves, regardless of their prior experience, and where the true potential of every employee can be realized.

In the final chapter, we will summarize the key takeaways from this book and offer a call to action. We will explore how individuals, organizations, and society as a whole can embrace the paradigm shift towards valuing potential and redefining success in the workplace. Together, let us unlock the untapped potential within individuals and shape a future where competence is not determined solely by experience, but by the willingness to learn and grow.

Chapter Seven
Embracing the Paradigm Shift

Throughout this book, we have explored the concept of valuing potential over experience in the hiring and onboarding process. We have discussed the limitations of relying solely on prior experience and highlighted the untapped potential that lies within individuals who possess the drive, motivation, and willingness to learn. In this final chapter, we will summarize the key takeaways and offer a call to action for individuals, organizations, and society as a whole to embrace this paradigm shift.

1. *Recognize the Limitations of Experience:* Experience is undoubtedly valuable, but it should not be the sole

determining factor in hiring decisions. Understand that experience alone does not guarantee competence or success. By acknowledging the limitations of experience, we open ourselves up to the possibilities of nurturing potential and tapping into new talent.

2. *Shift Mindsets and Overcome Biases:* Challenge traditional mindsets and biases that hinder the recognition of potential. Understand that individuals without extensive experience can bring fresh perspectives, enthusiasm, and a hunger for growth. Embrace diversity and inclusion, valuing the diverse talents and backgrounds that individuals with potential can bring to the table.

3. *Emphasize Qualities and Skills:* Focus on assessing qualities such as motivation, adaptability, curiosity, and communication skills during the hiring process. Look for candidates who exhibit a willingness to learn, grow, and collaborate. By prioritizing these qualities, organizations can create a workforce that is agile, innovative, and capable of adapting to change.

4. ***Design Comprehensive Onboarding Programs***: Invest in designing effective onboarding programs that nurture the potential of new hires. Provide clear expectations, mentorship, ongoing training, feedback mechanisms, and opportunities for collaboration. By creating a supportive environment that encourages continuous learning and growth, organizations empower individuals to reach their full potential.

5. ***Foster a Culture of Potential:*** Cultivate a culture that values and rewards growth, development, and the pursuit of potential. Recognize and celebrate achievements, milestones, and the efforts of individuals who have demonstrated exceptional growth. By creating a culture that prioritizes potential, organizations inspire employees to continuously strive for excellence.

6. ***Embrace Continuous Improvement:*** Constantly evaluate and refine hiring and onboarding processes to optimize the identification and cultivation of potential. Learn from experiences, seek feedback, and make necessary adjustments

to ensure the continuous growth and development of individuals within the organization.

As individuals, organizations, and society as a whole, let us embrace this paradigm shift and redefine success in the workplace. Let us value the potential of individuals, irrespective of their prior experience, and create a culture that encourages growth, innovation, and collaboration. By doing so, we unleash the power of untapped talent and shape a future where competence is not confined to the boundaries of experience but driven by the willingness to learn and adapt.

In conclusion, "Inexperienced, but not Incompetent" presents a compelling argument for rethinking traditional hiring practices and embracing the potential that lies within individuals who are eager to learn and contribute. By prioritizing qualities, fostering growth, and nurturing potential, we can create a more inclusive, dynamic, and successful workforce. Let us embark on this journey of transformation and unlock the limitless possibilities that lie within each individual.

Chapter Eight

A Future of Potential

In this final chapter, we look ahead to a future where the paradigm shift towards valuing potential has been fully embraced. We envision a world where the hiring and onboarding process focuses on the qualities that truly drive success and where individuals are given equal opportunities to prove their capabilities.

1. *A More Inclusive Workplace:* The shift towards valuing potential creates a more inclusive workplace that recognizes and celebrates the diversity of talent. Organizations actively seek out individuals from different backgrounds, experiences, and educational paths. By breaking down barriers, we create a workforce that reflects the rich tapestry of society and leverages the collective strengths and perspectives of its members.

2. *A Culture of Lifelong Learning:* Embracing potential means embracing the concept of lifelong learning. Organizations prioritize continuous development and provide ongoing training opportunities for employees at all stages of their

careers. Employees are encouraged to take ownership of their growth, supported by a learning culture that values curiosity, experimentation, and innovation.

3. *Nurturing Future Leaders:* By valuing potential, organizations identify and nurture future leaders early on. They invest in the growth and development of individuals, empowering them to take on greater responsibilities and lead with confidence. The emphasis shifts from simply assessing past achievements to recognizing leadership potential and providing the necessary support and mentorship to foster it.

4. *Thriving in an Evolving Landscape:* In a rapidly changing world, organizations that embrace potential are better equipped to adapt and thrive. They have a workforce that is agile, resilient, and capable of embracing new technologies, industries, and challenges. These organizations can navigate uncertainty with confidence, leveraging the potential within their teams to drive innovation and growth.

5. *Impact on Society:* The impact of valuing potential extends beyond individual organizations. As more companies adopt this approach, it ripples through society, challenging

traditional notions of success and reshaping the way we think about talent and competence. It creates opportunities for individuals who may have been overlooked in the past and paves the way for a more equitable and merit-based society.

In this future, potential is celebrated and nurtured. Organizations and individuals recognize that greatness is not solely determined by prior experience but by the willingness to learn, adapt, and grow. The success of individuals and organizations is measured by the impact they create and the value they bring to the table.

As we conclude this book, let us carry the message of valuing potential forward. Let us challenge the status quo, question biases, and champion a future where everyone has the opportunity to thrive. By embracing potential, we unlock a world of possibilities and create a future that is inclusive, dynamic, and filled with endless potential. Together, let us shape that future and build a world where the inexperienced are not seen as incompetent, but as capable individuals ready to make their mark.

Chapter Nine

Your Journey of Potential

In this final chapter, we turn our attention to you, the reader, and your own journey of potential. We have explored the importance of valuing potential in hiring and onboarding processes, but now it's time to apply these principles to your own life and career.

1. ***Embrace a Growth Mindset:*** Adopt a growth mindset, believing that your abilities and skills can be developed with effort and dedication. Recognize that your potential is not limited by your current experience or qualifications. Embrace challenges, seek out new opportunities, and approach setbacks as opportunities for learning and growth.

2. ***Define Your Personal Vision:*** Take the time to reflect on your personal vision and goals. What do you want to achieve? What skills do you want to develop? Define a clear vision for yourself and set specific, actionable goals that align with that vision. Break down those goals into smaller

steps and create a roadmap for your journey of growth and potential.

3. ***Continuously Learn and Develop:*** Commit to lifelong learning and development. Seek out opportunities to acquire new skills, whether through formal education, online courses, workshops, or hands-on experiences. Be proactive in expanding your knowledge and honing your abilities. Stay curious, stay open-minded, and embrace new challenges that push you outside your comfort zone.

4. ***Seek Mentors and Support:*** Surround yourself with mentors, coaches, and individuals who believe in your potential and can guide you along your journey. Seek out mentors who have experience and expertise in your desired field. Their insights and advice can be invaluable in helping you navigate challenges, build new skills, and unlock your potential.

5. ***Embrace Failure as a Stepping Stone:*** Don't be afraid of failure. Embrace it as a stepping stone on your journey of potential. Learn from your mistakes, adapt your approach, and keep moving forward. Failure is not an indication of incompetence but an opportunity for growth and resilience.

6. ***Stay Agile and Adaptable:*** In a rapidly changing world, agility and adaptability are essential. Embrace change, be open to new ideas, and be willing to pivot when necessary. The ability to adapt and learn quickly will set you apart and enable you to seize new opportunities that come your way.

7. ***Celebrate Your Achievements:*** Along your journey of potential, celebrate your achievements, no matter how small they may seem. Recognize your growth, acknowledge your progress, and take pride in your accomplishments. Celebrating milestones and successes reinforces your confidence and motivation to continue pushing forward.

Remember, your potential is limitless. It is not confined by your past experiences or the expectations of others. Embrace the power within you, believe in your abilities, and take bold steps towards your goals. Your journey of potential is unique and filled with opportunities for growth, learning, and success.

As we conclude this book, I invite you to take what you have learned and apply it to your own life and career. Embrace the paradigm shift of valuing potential, both in yourself and in others. Together, let us create a world where everyone has the opportunity to unleash their potential and make a lasting impact.

Thank you for joining me on this journey. May your path be filled with growth, fulfillment, and the realization of your untapped potential.

In addition to the previous chapters, it is crucial to acknowledge the importance of giving chances and opportunities to inexperienced individuals. By doing so, we open doors to discovering hidden talents and unlocking the potential that may have otherwise gone unnoticed. This not only benefits individuals but also contributes to creating a better world for both the inferior and superior masses.

In a society that values potential, it is essential to foster an environment of support and collaboration. By helping one another, we can assist individuals in discovering their purpose in life. Through mentorship, guidance, and sharing experiences, we can inspire and empower others to explore their passions, strengths, and unique contributions to the world.

By embracing the potential of both the experienced and inexperienced, we create a diverse and inclusive society that thrives on the collective strengths and talents of its members. Together, we can make our world a better place by creating opportunities, breaking down barriers, and recognizing the inherent value in every individual.

Ultimately, the journey towards a better world starts with each one of us. By valuing potential, embracing diversity, and supporting one another, we can create a more equitable and fulfilling society where everyone has the chance to discover their purpose and make a positive impact. Let us join hands and work together towards a future where untapped potential is recognized, nurtured, and celebrated.